AFFIRMING

Marty

INTRODUCING RICHARD HOOKER AND THE LAWS OF ECCLESIASTICAL POLITY

Series Editor: Jeffrey John

DARTON·LONGMAN+TODD

For the people of St Andrew's, Bedford
Catholic, Liberal and Creative

First published in 1999 by
Darton, Longman and Todd Ltd
1 Spencer Court
140–142 Wandsworth High Street
London SW18 4JJ

in association with

Affirming Catholicism
St Luke's Centre
90 Central Street
London EC1V 8AQ

ISBN 0-232-52317-7

The views expressed in this book are those of the author and do not
necessarily reflect any policy of Affirming Catholicism.

Designed and produced by Sandie Boccacci
in QuarkXPress on an Apple PowerMac
Set in 10/12^{1}/$_{2}$pt Times
Printed and bound in Great Britain by Page Brothers, Norwich

Affirming Catholicism

Affirming Catholicism is a movement (not an ecclesiastical party) which exists to do two things. We affirm our confidence in our Anglican heritage; and we seek to renew and promote the Catholic tradition within it. Our aim is to explore, explain and share with others both inside and outside the Church a lively, intelligent and inclusive Catholic faith. In the words of our Trust Deed:

> It is the conviction of many that a respect for scholarship and free enquiry has been characteristic of the Church of England and of the Churches of the wider Anglican Communion from earliest times, and is fully consistent with the status of those Churches as part of the Holy Catholic Church. It is desired to establish a charitable educational foundation which will be true both to those characteristics and to the Catholic tradition within Anglicanism ... The object of the foundation shall be the advancement of education in the doctrines and the historical development of the Church of England and the Churches of the wider Anglican Communion, as held by those standing within the Catholic tradition.

Our Publications

These are offered as one means of presenting Anglican Catholic teaching and practice in as clear and accessible a form as possible. Some cover traditional doctrinal and liturgical themes: others attempt to present a well-argued Catholic viewpoint on issues of debate currently facing the Church. There is a list of our series of booklets on page v.

The present series of books is provided, where appropriate, with summaries to sections and suggested questions which we hope will facilitate personal study or discussion in groups. Other most recent titles in the series are:

Anglican Orders and the Priesting of Women Paul Avis
Making a Rule of Life John Gaskell
The Practice of Abortion: A Critique Michael Banner

To order these publications individually or on subscription, or for further information about the aims and activities of Affirming Catholicism, write to:

> The Secretary
> Affirming Catholicism
> St Luke's Centre
> 90 Central Street
> London EC1V 8AQ
>
> Tel: 0171 253 1138
> Fax: 0171 253 1139

Books in the Affirming Catholicism series

About the Author

Martyn Percy is the Director of the Lincoln Theological Institute for the Study of Religion and Society, University of Sheffield. He is the author of *Words, Wonders and Power: Understanding Contemporary Christian Fundamentalism and Revivalism* (SPCK, 1966), *Intimate Affairs: Sexuality and Spirituality in Perspective* (Darton, Longman and Todd, 1997) and *Power and the Church: Ecclesiology in an Age of Transition* (Cassell, 1998)

Studies in Fundamentalism (SPCK), and *Previous Convictions: An Anatomy of Conversion* (SPCK) are shortly to be published. A new four-volume series published by Sheffield Academic Press – Lincoln Studies in Religion and Society – will shortly be available.

Canon Trevor Page is Director of Ordinands, Diocese of Sheffield.

Contents

Introducing Richard Hooker

Reading the works of Richard Hooker is not unlike trying to study the writings of Shakespeare and Kant simultaneously. It may (eventually) turn out to be a very rewarding experience, but it would require the full concentration of any scholar. Furthermore, a fifty-page introduction to *The Laws of Ecclesiastical Polity* could be likened to a one-sentence guide to a cathedral. Clearly, justice can never be done.

Nevertheless, the function of this small booklet is to acquaint the uninitiated, with ordinands especially being in mind, briefly with one of the foremost theologians and ecclesiologists of Anglicanism. In presenting such an account, I am conscious that few today have ever read Hooker. Even amongst ordinands, it is quite probable that the mention of his name will elicit an expression of puzzlement rather than a smile of recognition. And yet he is well known and well read by many Roman Catholics, scholars of rhetoric, historians and political scientists. Indeed, it is not an overstatement to suggest that it is virtually impossible to understand the Anglican Church without having some grasp of Hooker. So why do so few read his works, specifically *The Laws of Ecclesiastical Polity*?

Part of the answer must lie in the density of his language, which, to the unsuspecting reader, will appear forbidding at first sight. Hooker wrote prose that was remarkable for its clarity, grace and modernity: it was stately, dignified and rhythmic. Although a polemicist, he is first and foremost a theologian, and he adopts an extraordinary range of tone in the presentation of his arguments. He is sometimes ironic and sarcastic, although not usually in relation to his Puritan opponents, whom he treats with respect. As an advocate, he adopts a number of personae: teacher, critic, wise expounder (of maxims), respectful student (of the fathers and philosophers), fellow Christian, cleric and moderate nationalist.

For someone with time to spend, analysis of his writing reveals a person who understood the power of rhetoric and how to construct it for his own argument. There are short sentences – 'little daggers' as Cicero called them – which are invariably telling. Yet the more normative style of Hooker is long sentences. For example, Book 1 of *The Laws* has a sentence of two hundred and sixty-seven words; even the average number is forty-two. In Book 5 of *The Laws*, there is a sentence that exceeds five hundred words. Despite the density of the work, Hooker's prose is one of nobility and power, as he tries to win over his readers to wisdom through the simple offering of instruction, teaching and enlightenment.

I do not claim to be an expert on Hooker so much as an enthusiast. In any case, 'expertise' in Hooker is somewhat shared rather than concentrated, since he is a sufficiently substantial figure to be read in his own right by theologians, ecclesiologists, historians, analysts of rhetoric and political scientists. In fact, my initial acquaintance with Hooker was almost accidental. I discovered – in the course of some research into Anglican polity – that Hooker's father-in-law had been a Merchant Taylor (like myself), as was Lancelot Andrewes, whose preaching and writing I have long admired. Curious to know more, I began to read some of Hooker's sermons, and in due course, came to appreciate *The Laws of Ecclesiastical Polity*.

Today there is something of a renaissance amongst theologians in studying Hooker. A number of recent tomes on the nature of Anglicanism have sought to accentuate his importance for ecclesiology. There is a reasonably lively debate as to who can 'claim' Hooker as their champion: Catholics or Protestants? (Neither, I suspect – his magisterial *via media* is too complex for him to be owned by any one party.) The recent series *Cambridge Texts in the History of Political Thought* (edited by Arthur McGrade, CUP, 1989), have re-issued parts of The Laws, namely the Preface ('To them that seek ... the reformation of Laws ...'), Book 1 ('Concerning Laws and their severall kind in generale') and Book 8 ('On the power of Ecclesiastical Dominion as by *The Laws* of this Land belongeth unto the Supreme Regent ...'),

It is with some justice that C.S. Lewis described Hooker's writings as *architectonic*, built up into a huge and carefully constructed edifice: it is hard to quote well from such a work. It is hard to convey the majesty of a cathedral by focusing on one of its smaller stones. So the function of this booklet is to provide some insight into Hooker, and to offer a sample of his writings that will enthuse and inspire readers to delve further for themselves. Such an introduction cannot be comprehensive. But in outlining Hooker's thoughts on the Church, ministry, sacraments and Scriptures, the shape of his thinking and the context that formed it should become clearer for the first-time reader. This is the primary purpose of the Primer, and especially for ordinands.

In *The Laws of Ecclesiastical Polity*, we meet a writer who belongs to a kind of early English empiricism. These 'Laws' were never to be imposed uncritically or literalistically, but were rather 'discovered' and 'fashioned', as though sculpting from the finest materials. Hooker's legacy is the presentation of Anglicanism as a kind of system or craft, inculcating beauty, truth, politics, persuasion, logic, worship, tradition, faith, reason and feeling. And all of this is in the service of God, for the shaping of the Church and for the good of society.

REVD CANON DR MARTYN PERCY
Lincoln Theological Institute for the Study of Religion and Society, University of Sheffield
New Year 1999

Richard Hooker: Key Dates

1554 Richard Hooker born in late March, probably in Heavitree, a suburb of Exeter.

1562 John Jewel, Bishop of Salisbury, publishes his *Apologia*.

1568 Hooker enters Corpus Christi College, Oxford, having attended grammar school in Exeter.

1571 Death of Bishop Jewel, Hooker's early patron.

1579 Hooker becomes Fellow of his college.

1583 John Whitgift becomes Archbishop of Canterbury.

1584 Hooker appointed Vicar of Drayton-Beauchamp, Buckinghamshire.

1585 17 March, Hooker appointed Master of the Temple, London. Beginning of controversy with Walter Travers which lasted into 1586.

1588 February: Hooker marries Joan Churchman, in London.

1591 Hooker appointed to the parish of Boscombe, near Salisbury, as well as being Prebend of Netheravon.

1593 *Of the Laws of Ecclesiastical Polity*, Books 1–4, published.

1595 Hooker appointed Rector of Bishopsbourne.

1597 *Of the Laws of Ecclesiastical Polity*, Book 5, published.

1600 November 2, Hooker dies of complications following a chill.

1603 Death of Joan Hooker.

1612 Henry Jackson begins publication of Hooker's *Tractates and Sermons*, at the request of John Spenser.

1648 *Of the Laws of Ecclesiastical Polity*, Books 6 & 8 published.

1662 *Of the Laws of Ecclesiastical Polity*, Book 7, published in the first complete edition, with a biography by John Gauden.

1665 *Life of Richard Hooker* by Izaak Walton published.

Hooker's Life and Context

By the time Hooker was born in Heavitree, Exeter, in 1554, the founding fathers of the Reformation were either dead or about to die: Luther eight years earlier, Calvin eight years later. The Lutheran protest against the sale of indulgences had developed into a religiously-funded nationalist protest against papal authority, and a theological protest focused on the assertion of the doctrine of justification through faith received by grace. In Calvinism, the Reformation had developed a more austere mode, with a church order in Geneva dismissive of bishops, priests and deacons, discarding of traditional liturgies, and suspicious of sacramentalism.

The 1500s in England had seen several turbulent and violent chapters in its history of religious change. Under Henry VIII (1509-47) Catholicism had initially been endorsed, then Roman authority denied and monasteries dissolved. The years of Edward VI (1547-53) saw a more fundamental style of Protestantism: the continental reformers' doctrines could be taught, clergy might marry and images be removed. Cranmer's liturgy (*The Book of Common Prayer*) set out to conserve a catholicity from the past whilst reforming it along Protestant lines, and recasting it in the culture and language of seventeenth-century England.

From 1553 to 1558, Queen Mary made a forceful attempt to return to the form of Roman Catholicism that had existed before her father, Henry VIII. All religious legislation from the previous reign was repealed, the Prayer Book banned, and Cranmer burned with some 300 others. With the accession of Elizabeth I in 1558, a fresh attempt was made to reinstate reform, to allow Protestant teachings, yet not to deny catholicity in denying Roman authority. This endeavour was 'the Elizabethan Settlement': there was a wideness of mercy, and its text was Cranmer's Prayer Book.

Hooker grew up as a child of that settlement and became committed to it. But it was a fragile covenant. On the one hand there was the opposition of Catholics, perhaps epitomised by John Jewel (1522-71), Bishop of Salisbury, who argued for a Church based firmly on Catholic truth, claiming a continuity with the undivided Church of the early centuries (*Apologia Pro Ecclesia Anglicana*, 1562). Then there were Puritans, posing an array of threats clustered around congregationalism, literalism (in reading Scripture), and the dismantling of socio-ecclesial order. In his eight volumes of *The Laws of Ecclesiastical Polity*, Hooker was to defend the Church against the will of the Puritan reformers, a body of people so named not because of their actual moral purity, but because they sought to 'purify' and ultimately purge the Church of much of its tradition.

Hooker was ordained a priest in 1582, aged twenty-eight. He is colourfully portrayed by Izaak Walton, his biographer, as a man of reticence and modesty. Actually, he was more than this, and although Walton's gentle hagiography is a beautiful testimony to a great man, Walton sometimes obscures the reality in his portrayal of piety. For example, Walton misses the sense of humour that can be detected in Hooker's writings. Walton also seems to suggest that Hooker had an impoverished marriage, which I suspect is a literary device to connote his forbearance. In actual fact, Joan Churchman (Hooker's wife) was the daughter of a Merchant Taylor, and the family were in all probability reasonably well off.

From 1568 until 1584, Hooker was at Corpus Christi, Oxford, first as a student and then as a Fellow. Walton describes Hooker's time at Oxford in glowing terms:

> [He] had by a constant unwearied diligence attained unto a perfection in all the learned languages; by the help of

which, an excellent tutor, and his unintermitted studies, he had made the subtlety of all the arts easy and familiar to him, and useful for the discovery of such learning as lay hid from common searchers; so that by these added to his great reason, and his industry added to both, he did not only know more of causes and effects; but what he knew, he knew better than other men.

(Walton's *Life and Death*, 1665, 1:14)

Walton adds that in four years, he missed the college chapel prayers only twice. He further reports that in his studies, Hooker enriched his

quiet and capacious soul with the precious learning of the philosophers, casuists, and schoolmen; and with them, the foundation and reason of all laws, both sacred and civil ... And as he was diligent in these, so he seemed restless in searching the scope and intention of God's Spirit revealed to mankind in the sacred scripture ... And the good man would often say, that 'God abhors confusion as contrary to his nature;' and as often say, that 'the scripture was not writ to beget disputations and pride, and opposition to government; but moderation, charity and humility, obedience to authority, and peace to mankind: of which virtues,' he would as often say 'no man did ever repent himself upon his death-bed.' (Walton, 1:18-19)

As for his behaviour towards others, Walton suggests that

it is observable that he was never known to be angry, or passionate, or extreme in any of his desires; never heard to repine or dispute with Providence, but, by a quiet gentle submission and resignation of his will to the wisdom of his Creator, bore the burthen [burden] of the day with patience; never heard to utter an uncomely word; and by this, and a grave behaviour, which is a divine charm, he begot an early reverence unto his person, even from those

that at other times, and in other companies, took a liberty
to cast off that strictness of behaviour and discourse that
is required in collegiate life. (Walton, 1:15)

The first part of this is only half true. It is clear that Hooker
was a passionate exponent of his views, and on many an
occasion could be very sharp in his writings: it is a mistake
to stress the irenic over the ironic. While Walton wrote in
hagiographic tones, and revered Hooker in ways that seem
out of touch with today (as he did with the subjects of his
other biographies), his words should be seen as intention-
ally complementing what Hooker had come to stand for:
patient scholarship, a depth of learning and a genuine and
perhaps unique skill in ecclesiology. Walton was writing at
a distance – sixty-five years after Hooker's death to be exact –
and we should be careful about presuming too much on his
views. So, the description of Hooker as living in tight
domestic circumstances yet 'possessing his soul in patience
and peace', should be seen as contributing to a portrait of
restraint and moderation. Here is a picture of patience, as a
response to continual problems that are often close to the
core of what Anglican parochial ministry is taken to be, at
its best. Hooker had a brief experience of this, for in 1584
he became Vicar of Drayton-Beauchamp, near Aylesbury.
But it was to be short-lived, for in a matter of months, fresh
challenges were encountered that influenced the remainder
of his life.

In March 1585 Hooker was appointed as Master of the
Temple for the Inns of Court in London. It was a fraught
appointment (following the death of Dr Richard Alvey, a
noted Puritan), with the leading candidate for the post being
Walter Travers. Elizabeth's Chancellor, Lord Burghley,
strongly supported the candidature of Travers; but it was
sunk by a sharp missive fired by Whitgift, Archbishop of
Canterbury, who wrote to the Queen describing Travers as
'an earnest seeker after innovation'. Whitgift's own first

choice was too sick to take the post. Hooker was Whitgift's second, and the Queen appointed him.

The description applied to Travers was a code for indicating him to be a Puritan. A continental reformation based on Luther's prescription that the Church should not perpetuate any practice to which Scripture was demonstrably opposed was now fused to a new conviction that nothing at all should be done unless provable from Scripture. It was a tide of opinion which swept through the Elizabethan Church, making the borders with continental Protestantism indistinct, questioning the identity of the Church.

It was this form of Puritanism that Hooker was to set his face against. Yet Hooker was to encounter considerable opposition. Travers was a radical reformer. Worse, for Hooker, he was also a lecturer and preacher at the Temple. After a sermon by Hooker, Travers appealed to the Privy Council (sometime in 1590), accusing Hooker of claiming God to be merciful to Romanists, who might place more emphasis on works rather than justification by faith.

It was to escape the worst exertions of such controversy that Hooker sought to leave the Mastership for a return to parish ministry. Yet he also wished to devote a great proportion of his time in the parish to take part in that controversy by writing *The Laws of Ecclesiastical Polity*. From 1591-5 he was Rector of Boscombe, Subdean of Salisbury and a Prebend of Netheravon. From there, Books 1–4 were published in 1593. In 1595 he moved to Bishopsbourne, near Canterbury, where Book 5 was published in 1597. Books 6–8 were completed before Hooker's death – on 2 November 1600. But manuscripts were lost, and the books as we now have them are later constructions based on some notes and earlier drafts. Books 6 and 8 were not published until 1648, and Book 7 until 1662, the year of the Restoration.

To what extent have these books mattered to others?

They sold slowly during Hooker's lifetime. Whitgift, to whom they were dedicated, clearly read them. Pope Clement VIII was a reluctant reader of English books, claiming 'never to have met with an English book whose writer deserved the name of an author'. But he had some of Book 1 read to him in Latin and concluded (according to Walton) '...this man indeed deserves the name of an author. Most books will get reverence by age for there is in them such seeds of eternity that if the rest be like this they shall last till the last fire consumes all learning.' *The Laws* were studied by Charles I who enjoined his son to do likewise. Indeed they were hugely influential on the development of Anglican thought in the Caroline period with Laud, Lancelot Andrewes, John Donne, Bishop Cosin and Jeremy Taylor finding Hooker to ecclesiology what Cranmer was to liturgy. As we have already noted, there is plenty to admire. In a typical passage, Hooker adopts a characteristic modesty that would grace any theology:

> Dangerous it were for the feeble brain of man to wade far into the doings of the Most High; whom although to know be life, and joy to make mention of his name; yet our soundest knowledge is to know that we know him not as indeed he is, neither can know him; and our safest eloquence concerning him is our silence, when we confess without confession that his glory is inexplicable, his greatness above our capacity and reach. He is above, and we upon earth; therefore it behoveth our words to be wary and few. (Book 1. II.2)

The eighteenth century was a quieter one, with no fresh publications between 1723 and 1793. Modern publications received their impetus from a superbly annotated edition edited by John Keble between 1836 and 1841. Other editions followed. Richard Church and Francis Paget revised the Keble edition in 1888, and Everyman produced a popular version of Books 1-5 in 1907. This century has seen a complete Folger Library edition published in the USA, although it is very expensive to acquire. The text that is used in this booklet is taken from the Everyman edition (edited by Christopher Morris, J.M. Dent, London: 1954 impression). The material quoted from Book 8 of *The Laws* comes from the Cambridge (1989) text, edited by Arthur McGrade.

The Laws of Ecclesiastical Polity:
A Brief Outline

The word 'polity' suggests both form, a system of government, and process: how governing is done. It is suggestive of policy (yet more basic), elucidating the grounds on which policy may be made, and more widely, pointing to the means by which policy is carried out. The aims of *The Laws of Ecclesiastical Polity* are clear: to defend 'the present state of the Church of God established among us.' Hooker's work is an apologia for an ecclesiology that is faithful to both Catholicism and the Reformation, and yet cannot be owned by either of these extremes. It so happens that the defence Hooker adopts is mainly against congregationally-centred Puritanism. Although he reserves his formal theological refutation of Puritanism and the defence of episcopacy for Books 6 and 7 of *The Laws*, the very tenor of the Preface suggests this agenda – namely the dangers of Puritanism – is on his mind from the very beginning:

> The Church of Christ is a body mystical. A body cannot stand unless the parts thereof be proportionable. Let it therefore be required at both parts, at the hands of the clergy, to be in meanness of state like the Apostles; at the hand of the laity, to be as they were who lived under the Apostles: and in this reformation there will be, though little wisdom, yet some indifferency.
>
> But your reformation which are of the clergy (if yet it displeases you not that I should say that ye are of the clergy) seemeth to aim at a broader mark. Ye think that he which will perfectly reform must bring the form of church-discipline unto the state which then it was at. A

thing neither possible, nor certain, nor absolutely convenient.

Concerning the first, what was used in the Apostles' times, the Scripture fully declareth not; so that making their times the rule and canon of church-polity, ye make a rule, which being not possible to be fully known, is as impossible to be kept.

Again, sith the latter even of the Apostles' own times had that which in the former was not thought upon; in this general proposing of the Apostolical times, there is no certainty which should be followed: especially seeing that ye give us great cause to doubt how far ye allow these times. (Pref. IV. 3-4)

Overall, the Preface – nine 'chapters' in actual fact – engages with great wit and tenacity against the Puritan claim that church life should be based only on what is demonstrably proven by scriptural precedent. This endeavour, argues Hooker, is wrongly conceived and impossible to carry out. Moreover, Hooker is anxious to refute these 'spiritual credentials' – even though he considers them erroneous – for he detects behind them the hand of separatism; and behind that, socially subversive implications for Elizabethan society. He appeals to Puritans directly:

The best and safest way for you therefore, my dear brethren, is, to call your deeds past to a new reckoning, to re-examine the cause ye have taken in hand, and to try it even point by point, argument by argument, with all the diligent exactness ye can; to lay aside the gall of that bitterness wherein your minds have hitherto over-bounded, and with meekness to search for the truth. Think ye are men, deem it not impossible for you to err; sift unpartially your own hearts, whether it be force of reason or vehemency of affection, which hath bred and still doth feed these opinions in you. If truth do any where manifest itself, seek not to smother it with glossing delusions, acknowledge the greatness thereof, and think it your best victory when the same doth prevail over you.

(Pref. IX. 1)

Book 1 is a discussion of the nature of law, or rather of a set of interconnected laws, from the laws by which God's divine life is ordered to those which govern the detail of civil transactions. Books 2 and 3 return to the debate with the Puritans over the interpretation of Scripture and the place of reason in interpretation. Hooker expresses the substance of his argument for Books 1-3 like this:

Wherefore seeing that laws and ordinances in particular, whether such as we observe, or such as yourselves would have established; - when the mind doth sift and examine them, it must needs have often recourse to a number of doubts and questions about the nature, kinds and qualities of laws in general; whereof unless it be thoroughly informed, there will appear no certainty to stay our persuasion upon: I have for that cause set down in the first place an introduction on both sides needful to be considered: declaring therein what law is, how different kinds of law there are, and what force they are of according unto each kind.

This done, because ye suppose the laws for which ye strive are found in the Scripture, but those not against which ye strive; and upon this surmise are drawn to hold it as the very main pillar of your whole cause, 'That Scripture ought to be the only form of all our actions', and consequently that the church-orders which we observe being not commanded in Scripture, are offensive and displeasant unto God: I have spent the second Book in sifting of this point, which standeth with you for the first and chiefest principle whereon ye build.

Whereunto the next in degree is, That as God will have always a church upon earth, while the world doth continue, and that church stand in need of government; of which government it behoveth Himself to be both the Author and Teacher: so it cannot stand with duty that man should ever presume in any wise to change and alter the same; and therefore 'that in Scripture there must of necessity be found some particular form of Polity Ecclesiastical, the Laws whereof admit not any kind of alteration'. (Pref. VII. 2-4)

In Book 4 there is a defence of Anglican liturgical practices taken over from Rome, as being not of their essence 'Romish', but belonging as catholic and universal elements of the true Church.

The first three books being thus ended, the fourth proceedeth from the general grounds and foundations of your cause unto your general accusations against us, as having in the orders of our church (for so you pretend) 'corrupted the right form of church-polity with manifold popish rites and ceremonies, which certain reformed churches have banished from amongst them, and thereby have given us such an example as' (you think) 'we ought to follow'. This your assertion hath herein drawn us to make search, whether these be just exceptions against the customs of our church, when ye plead that they are the same that the church of Rome hath, or that they are not the same which some other reformed churches have devised. (Pref. VII. 5)

Book 5 is by far the longest and is also the most powerful as a piece of literature. It can be seen as one great extended commentary on *The Book of Common Prayer*. It is concerned with the detail of worship (including discussions on baptism, chanting and ministerial attire), with sacramental theology, and with the principles which should govern change in worship:

> Of those four books which remain and are bestowed about the specialities of that cause which lieth in controversy, the first [i.e., Book 5] examineth the causes by you alleged, wherefore the public duties of Christian religion, as our prayers, our Sacraments, and the rest, should not be ordered in such sort as with us they are; nor that power, whereby the persons of men are consecrated unto the ministry, be disposed of in such manner as the laws of this church do allow. (Pref. VII. 6)

Book 6 is claimed to be about lay leadership, but is much more about the justification and practice of penitence. Book 7 is a defence of episcopacy, and Book 8 concerns the Royal Supremacy and the place of the Crown in the Church. Again, Hooker summarises:

> The second and third [i.e., Books 6 and 7] are concerning the power of jurisdiction: the one, whether laymen, such as your governing elders are, ought in all congregations for ever to be invested with that power; the other, whether bishops may have that power over other pastors, and therewithal that honour, which with us they have? And because besides the power of order which all consecrated persons have, and the power of jurisdiction which neither they all nor they only have, there is a third power, a power of ecclesiastical domination, communicable, as we think, unto persons not ecclesiastical, and most fit to be restrained unto the Prince or Sovereign commander over the whole body politic: the eighth Book we have allotted unto this question, and have sifted therein your objections against those preeminences royal wherein thereunto appertain. (Pref. VII. 6)

In conclusion, it must be stressed that although Hooker seeks to win over his audience, he does so with the ultimate intention of reconciliation and unity. The Puritan threat vexed him, but the manner of his dialogue and argument set a standard and bench-mark for conduct in theological disputes. Hooker wanted to see a united Church – the acme of the Elizabethan settlement – in which difference was allowed to flourish, provided that it did not lead to separatism, whilst neither retreating into a catholic past. In some ways, it would be reasonably fair to read him as a kind of forerunner to ecclesial liberalism. He is respectful of tradition, reason, 'the senses' and of Scripture, and he allows each of these to participate freely in debates. His view of Scripture is high, but he is an anti-literalist. The context in which he wrote demanded skilful rhetoric, deep intellect and genuine diplomacy. His conclusion to the Preface sets the tone:

> But our trust in the almighty is, that with us contentions are now at their highest float, and the day will come (for what cause of despair is there) when the passions of former enmity being allayed, we shall with ten times redoubled tokens of our unfeignedly reconciled love, show ourselves each towards other the same which Joseph and the brethren of Joseph were at the time of their interview in Egypt. Our comfortable expectation and most thirsty desire whereof what man soever amongst you shall in any way help to satisfy (as we truly hope there is no one amongst you but some way or other will) the blessings of the God of peace both in this world and in the world to come, be upon him more than the stars of the firmament in number. (Pref. IX. 4)

Reading Richard Hooker

In a postmodern age, a book about law in relation to theology might at first sight seem archaic. After all, in a (Western) post-foundational context in which reflexivity, difference and pragmatism are part of a new civic (or public) morality, 'laws' somehow seem inflexible, and perhaps even incapable of addressing our own times. To see laws like this, however, is to misunderstand the term, and certainly to misconstrue the rich way in which Hooker brings his concept of law to bear upon the Church. Hooker, as a Master of the Temple and as a theologian, develops his theories of principles in ways that are cognate with his public and ecclesial interests. Hooker does not believe in laws as though they were all divine dictats: nor are they faxes from heaven. Although there is a 'givenness' about some laws, others are to be discovered, crafted and worked with. Hooker's discussion of law lays the foundation for his theology and ecclesiology, and from the very beginning, it is clear that he is a moderate pluralist.

The purpose of this section cannot be to present any kind of comprehensive account of *The Laws*. Hooker's works – sermons, books and tracts – run to over 1500 pages. By nature, this booklet is attempting to show something of the beauty of his writing and, more specifically, to demonstrate how Hooker can still be called upon in today's Anglican Church. This is not in any way to claim Hooker for one party against another; as I have already said, he is too broad and complex to be owned by any one wing of the Church. That said, however, Hooker did write within a context, and *The Laws* represent a concerned attempt to address a kind of narrow theological and moral agenda that was at once both revolutionary and conservative. There are parallels today, as there have been in nearly every generation.

What is perhaps so enticing about Hooker's *Laws* is that they appear to be peculiarly well suited in speaking to the reflexive and post-foundational situation I mentioned earlier. In an age when the Bible has slipped (culturally) from being a rule book to a Guidebook, and where any legitimate authority is at the mercy of deconstruction and philosophies of suspicion, the Anglican Church needs sturdy theological resources that can address the present cultural situation and speak with integrity. Hooker, when judiciously and selectively read, can provide such a foundation. But how is it that one writing four hundred years ago can be so used? The answer, to an extent, lies in the expansive framework Hooker conceives for the operation of God in the world.

What follows, therefore, is a very small sample of his writing, with some brief comment. The selection is intended to demonstrate the width of Hooker's interests, but also to show that Hooker's concerns and context are not so very different from those of today. Hooker sought to construct a polity – rich in ecclesiology and theology – that embraced the very people his apologia is directed towards. They were separatists, literalists, schismatics, over-zealous reformers, and even sometimes rationalists; Hooker appeals to all. Comprehensiveness, in every sense, is Hooker's hallmark. He is liberal, catholic, evangelical and more besides. Beyond this, he offers a classic form of public theology, skilfully articulating a braiding and interweaving of religion, society, spirituality, politics, morality and individuality. All of this is in the interests of a common good that not only reflects and raises the status of society, but ultimately witnesses to a common God.

The Provision of Law and Scripture

Book 1 of *The Laws* is entitled 'Concerning Lawes, and their severall kindes in generall'. The book is careful to point out that there are different types of law (with different weights that can be brought to bear on varying matters), but that all laws are part of a generous and gracious economy provided by God:

> ... The being of God is a kind of law to his working; for that perfection which God is, giveth perfection to that he doth. Those natural, necessary, and internal operations of God, the Generation of the Son, the Proceeding of the Spirit, are without the compass of my present intent: which is to touch only such operations as have their beginning and being by a voluntary purpose, wherewith God hath eternally decreed when and how they should be. Which eternal decree is that which we term an eternal law.

> (Book 1.I.2)

Hooker is well aware that laws, and the institutions that implement them, are often not popular. His well-known remarks at the beginning of Book 1 concede as much: 'he that goeth about to persuade a multitude, that they are not so well-governed as they ought to be, shall never want attentive and favourable hearers...' (Book 1.I.1). Hooker also acknowledges that defenders of 'the Establishment' (as Hooker mostly is) are always at the mercy of reformers, since those in power are portrayed as self-serving.

However, Hooker wonders if the new 'laws' of Puritanism will be any better than the existing order he seeks to defend. According to C.S. Lewis, the greatest danger from Puritanism is what he described as 'Barthian reductiveness' (*English Literature in the Sixteenth Century Excluding Drama*, Oxford, Clarendon Press, 1954, p. 453), echoing Hooker's concern that 'your discipline being...the absolute commandment of almighty God, it must be received although the world by receiving it should be clean turned upside down...' (Pref. 8.5). It is with typical foresight (almost precognition if one thinks of the English Civil War or Revolution), that Hooker sees the dangers of all revolutions. In the name of liberation come new laws based on (apparently) sound moral and political principles, doing away with the old order. And yet the new laws can quickly turn out to be more faulty, narrow and pernicious than those that they were set to overthrow.

In view of this, Hooker locates the ground of being for his laws, not in a text, or in an ideology such as liberty or fraternity, nor indeed any other principle, but in the doctrine of the Trinity:

> Our God is one, but rather very Oneness, and mere unity, having nothing but itself in itself, and not consisting (as all things do besides God) of many things. In which essential Unity of God a Trinity personal nevertheless subsisteth, after a manner far exceeding the possibility of man's conceit. The works which outwardly are of God, they are in such sort of him being one, that each person hath in them somewhat peculiar and proper. For being Three, and they all subsisting in the essence of one Deity; from the Father, by the Son, through the Spirit, all things are. That which the Son doth hear of the Father, and which the Spirit doth receive of the Father and the Son, the same we have at the hands of the Spirit as being the last, and therefore the nearest unto us in order, although in power the same with the second and the first.
>
> (Book 1. II. 2)

This, it seems to me, casts the die for the unity and plurality that Hooker wishes to expound. There is a vision of communion and community, difference and unity that underpins

Hooker's fundamental understanding of laws. As such, there is one kind of law ('the first law eternal') which is the law of God's own being or purpose. The second kind of law is what might be loosely termed 'natural': 'that which with himself he hath set down as expedient to be kept by all his creatures' (Book 1.III.1). It is from this second type of law that all others flow, and Hooker then proceeds to categorise them: those laws which angels obey, those concerning humanity, reason, scriptural law, human law, and finally, laws of 'commonweal' (his term for the totality of an organic society), politic societies and nations.

For Hooker, laws are causal. *The Laws of Ecclesiastical Polity* are, in one way, a single self-conscious and systematic call for the Church to recognise that the operations of God are not simply confined to written rules, but are also known in works, practice and nature, the measure of them being their 'goodness'.

This treatment of law governs Hooker's handling of Scripture, placing it in a well-conceived double-bind. On the one hand, Hooker affirms that Scripture has a sacred authority; on the other, he acknowledges that Scripture cannot teach this itself, as it is a matter of faith and reason. Correspondingly, doctrines such as the Trinity are 'in scripture nowhere to be found by express literal mention, only deduced they are out of scripture by collection' (Book 1.XIV.2). Once again, we find Hooker critiquing literalism whilst holding to a form of authority which acquires a kind of otherness. Thus, the laws that govern the Church are any 'directive or rule unto goodness of operation' (Book 1.VIII.4). The expansion of the term of law reaches its peak in these words:

> All things that are, have some operation not violent or casual. Neither doth any thing ever begin to exercise the same without some fore-conceived end for which it worketh. And the end which it worketh for is not obtained, unless the work be also fit to obtain it by. For

unto every end every operation will not serve. That which doth assign unto each thing the kind, that which doth moderate the force and power, that which doth appoint the form and measure of working, the same we term a Law. (Book 1.II.1)

Hooker's perspective on law leads him to conclude that all laws, in their goodness, are derived from God. Furthermore, that understanding of laws (again in relation to theology) enables us to judge whether they are reasonable, righteous and just. The weighing of laws is a complex task for the Church, but also a rewarding one: ultimately, it is an enquiry into the grace of God. And Hooker's task throughout Book 1 is to broaden the understanding of law in the face of Puritan attempts to narrow it; for to do so is also to enlarge the vision of God.

In terms of interpreting Scripture, it may be useful here to make a distinction between literalism and fundamentalism. The former is very common, and may occur in almost any belief system: it describes a relationship between an individual or community, a text or ideology, and then a given situation; in other words, a kind of 'shadow trilateral'. Fundamentalism is normally more systematic and dogmatic, and will have an exclusive programme coupled to an outlook that is supported by articles of faith. Hooker is worried that Puritan literalism will eventually lead to 'fundamentalism' (although the term itself is a modern one). Hooker's antidote to this drift is to appeal to the depth and breadth of tradition (as well as human agency), not just Scripture. Here he is in agreement with the catholic theologians of the next generation, who criticised 'the Protestant dogma of the sufficiency and clarity of scripture – how do [they] know what scripture is *without* tradition?' Hooker would surely have affirmed the later Caroline attacks on 'bibliolatry', such as those penned by Samuel Fisher: 'the reduction of biblical writers to stenographers of the Spirit makes them no better than Balaam's ass' (Fisher, writing in 1660, against the Quaker John Owen, and his *Of the Divine, Original, Authority, Self-Evidencing Light, and the Power of Scriptures*, 1659).

Thus, Hooker's charge is that the Puritans think that 'the only law which God hath appointed to men in that behalf is sacred scripture'. He meets this with a simple affirmation, that even as we 'breathe, sleep, move, we set forth the glory of God', and that even 'the law of reason doth somewhat direct men how to honour God as their Creator' (Book 1. XVI. 5). In other words, there are more laws than those in the Scriptures, and all individuals and societies are governed by a plethora of beneficent higher powers, which are set down by God 'above every soul'. Hooker's teaching about the trio of Scripture, tradition and reason should be seen within the broader context of the provision of law. Naturally, in Hooker's mind, Scripture has some primacy, but as we have seen, it is not complete. Moreover, the primacy of Scripture is relational to, and complementary with, reason and tradition. In turn, these terms must be understood as having slightly different meanings then as now. Ultimately, Hooker would see all reason as needing to be infused with the Spirit as it seeks to work in the life of the Church and for the world.

Human Being

According to Hooker, humanity seeks the perfection of God through such things as the desire for immortality, community (including families), for constancy, for beauty and truth, for wisdom and virtue. Hooker is, in one sense, reclaiming Aquinas for Protestant Anglicanism. That is to say, he sees humanity as tending towards the fullness of a potential that lies beyond our unaided means to attain. Appropriately, humanity seeks development through knowledge: 'The soul of man being therefore at the first as a book, wherein nothing is, and yet all things may be imprinted; we are to search by what steps and degrees it riseth unto perfection of knowledge' (Book 1.VI.1). This phrase 'perfection of knowledge' is a key to Hooker's understanding of humanity and society. For Hooker, individuals and societies are redeemed through a process of completion as they correspond to the glory of God that is revealed in Christ, Creation and the Church.

Hooker does not appear to presuppose, in a narrow way, that human beings can be nothing without God. His view of humanity is altogether more positive, based on a much broader doctrine of God than the Puritan one he is writing against. Again, in a remarkable passage, Hooker expresses his belief that human beings can begin to acquire knowledge through sensation: then through natural reason, and finally through God:

> Man doth seek a triple perfection, first, a sensual, consisting in those things which very life itself requireth either as necessary supplements, or as beauties and ornaments thereof; then an intellectual, consisting in those things which none underneath man is either capable of or acquainted with; lastly a spiritual and divine, consisting in those things whereunto we tend by supernatural means here, but cannot here attain unto them. (Book 1.XI.4)

This is most suggestive, chiming as it does with the generic and modern Anglican quadrilateral. It was Schleiermacher (*The Christian Faith*, 1822), who posited that religion was 'a feeling of absolute dependence', which had eventually resulted in the expansion of the traditional Anglican trilateral (Scripture, tradition, reason) to include 'culture' or 'feelings'. Whilst Hooker would probably not have shared this perception, it is certainly interesting to see attention to 'the sensual' as a critical part of humanity's search and appreciation for God.

In a similarly 'naturalistic' account for moral action and principles, Hooker assumes that humanity has an inherent need to act; an impulse to action that is derived from God. In Book 2, in a passage on human action, Hooker's words resonate with the Gospel of Matthew, chapter 25:

> We move, we sleep, we take the cup at the hand of our friend, a number of things we oftentime do, only to satisfy some natural desire, without present, express, and actual reference unto any commandment of God. Unto his glory even these things are done which we naturally perform, and not only that which morally and spiritually we do. For by every effect proceeding from the most concealed instincts of nature His power is made manifest. But it doth not therefore follow that of necessity we shall sin, unless we expressly intend this in every such particular. (Book 2.II.1)

Also derived from God is the capacity of acting through choice: 'that (which) we do unto any such end, the same we choose and prefer before the leaving of it undone' (Book 1.VII.2). All human action, then, springs from knowledge and from will, which is almost synonymous with choice. It is this choice that must be constantly and appropriately directed, 'that all things must be done to the glory of God'. The search for God is a pilgrimage, and the pursuit of knowledge a pearl of great price. In this passage, Hooker seems to be suggesting that sin lies in ignorance and virtue in knowledge. Therefore, education is the key:

> Therefore that where we stand blameable, and can no way excuse it, is in doing evil, we prefer a less good before a greater, the greatness whereof is by reason investigable, and may be known. The search of knowledge is a thing painful; and the painfulness of knowledge is that which make the Will so hardly inclinable thereunto.

The root hereof, divine malediction; whereby the instruments being weakened wherewithal the soul (especially in reasoning) doth work, it preferreth rest in ignorance before wearisome labour to know. (Book 1.VII.7)

Hooker's remedy for this condition within humanity is to agree with the Apostle Paul – 'cast off all that presseth down; watch; labour; strive to go forward, and to grow in knowledge.'

Church and Society
Hooker was committed to a vision of Church and State that would generally be regarded as organic. That is to say, he saw their development as a matter of progressive growth and mutual interdependence, with Church and society providing one another with life and health. Organic approaches to ecclesiology recognise the heterogeneity of congregations and Churches, and their deep need to be reconciled in a common, if complicated life. For Hooker, the Church was a living body that was rooted in society, and sometimes in their operations, the two could not be distinguished. Church and society, like a robust and shady tree, or a fine mansion, are to provide a canopy under which all can live:

The stateliness of houses, the goodlines of trees, when we behold them delighteth the eye; but that foundation which beareth up the one, that root which ministereth unto the other nourishment and life, is in the bosom of the earth concealed: and if there be at any time occasion to search into it, such labour is then more necessary than pleasant, both to them which undertake it, and for lookers-on. In like manner the use and benefit of good laws, all that live under them may enjoy with delight and comfort, albeit the grounds and first original causes from whence they have sprung be unknown, as to the greatest part of men they are. (Book 1. I. 2)

In Hooker's mind, sociality is supported by two foundations

(or perhaps lives under two 'sacred canopies') – 'a natural inclination, whereby all men desire sociable life and fellowship' and 'an order expressly or secretly agreed upon, touching the manner of their union in living together' (Book 1.X.1). The agreed order is described by Hooker as 'the law of a Commonweal'. Significantly, the concept of an original agreement makes the order similar to a social contract. Hooker assumes that at a definite time people gathered to establish the social contract, and that they took the idea of 'family' as their basic model.

The concept of 'family' influences Hooker's ecclesial and social vision. In several places, society and Church are linked to the notion of 'roots', 'branches', parental motifs and kinship. Organic ecclesiologies are often characterised by mutuality, participation and partnership, even where a natural or revealed hegemony exists. Although Hooker is clear about legitimate authority, he is never draconian. Indeed, in some ways, he is surprisingly in tune with our own times.

> That which we spake before concerning the power of government must here be applied unto the power of making laws whereby to govern; which power God hath over all; and by the natural law whereunto he hath made all subject, the lawful power of making laws to command whole politic societies...belongeth so properly unto the same entire societies, that for any Prince or potentate of what kind soever upon earth to exercise the same of himself and not either by express commission immediately and personally received from God, or else by authority derived at the first from their consent upon whose persons they impose laws, it is no better then than mere tyranny.
>
> (Book 1.X.8)

Just as all types of law derive from divine laws, all authority derives from ultimate authority, which is from God. And yet Hooker does not abuse this lineage by demanding slavish obedience. Laws are public, and truth is in a kind of common trusteeship. The passage suggests, at least indirectly, that consent of the governed is necessary for laws to be implemented. Furthermore, it states that in English society Parliament is the normal body for making laws, just as councils are in churches.

Doctrine in Worship: Baptism and Eucharist

Hooker understood that a genuinely catholic Church would be innovative. He had little time for Puritans who would not countenance anything that was not enshrined in Scripture. Equally, he was set against a kind of traditionalism that prevented the Church adapting. Substantial parts of Book 5 are taken up with apparently trivial matters – the attire of ministers, music in church, architecture and the manner for administering sacraments. Yet for Hooker, these concerns arise directly out of his conviction that the Church, in its doctrine, preaching, practice and teaching, has some degree of leeway for adapting culturally and temporally. It was obvious to Hooker that Church polity need not be *in* Scripture, as much as it was obvious to him that it must not be *against* it. Thus, he writes that:

> Seeing therefore those canons do bind as they are edicts of nature, which the Jews observing as yet unwritten, and thereby framing such church orders as in their law were not prescribed, are not withstanding in that respect unculpable: it followeth that sundry things may be lawfully done in the Church, so as they be not done against the Scripture, although no Scripture do command them, but the Church only following the light of reason, judge them to be in discretion meet. (Book 3.VII. 2)

The authority given to reason here is not the elevation of rationality so much as the recognition of the place of common sense. It may well be that certain aspects of the life of the Church do not occur in the New Testament. But their absence does not invalidate their efficacy, since the laws of God (which are for goodness) are part of an ongoing organic Church that is imbued with the presence of God.

So, in addressing an issue such as lay women performing emergency baptisms, Hooker is typically charitable and pragmatic, letting common sense inform the situation rather than quoting spurious scriptures, or deducing dubious principles from the silence of the Fathers:

> But to women's baptism in private by occasion of urgent necessity, the reasons that only concern ordinary baptism in public are no just prejudice, neither can we by force thereof disprove the practise of those churches which (necessity requiring) allow baptism in private to be administered by women. We may not from laws that prohibit any thing with restraint conclude absolute and unlimited prohibitions. Although we deny not but they which utterly forbid such baptism may have perhaps wherewith to justify their orders against it. For even things lawful are well prohibited, when there is fear lest they make the way to unlawful more easy. And it may be the liberty of baptism by women at such times doth sometimes embolden the rasher sort to do it where no such necessity is. (Book 5. LXII. 2)

In Book 5, the vision of God – which has underpinned all laws – begins to mature in the various descriptions of the sacraments and the general conduct of ecclesial life:

> Sacraments are the powerful instruments of God to eternal life. For as our natural life consisteth in the union of the body with the soul; so our life supernatural in the union of the soul with God. And forasmuch as there is no union of God with man without that mean between both which is both, it seemeth requiste that we first consider how God is in Christ, then how Christ is in us, and how

the sacraments do serve to make us partakers of Ch
(Book 5.L.

In the specific case of the Eucharist:

> The bread and cup are his body and blood because they
> are causes instrumental upon the receipt whereof the par-
> ticipation of his body and blood ensueth. For that which
> produceth any certain effect is not vainly nor improperly
> said to be that very effect whereunto it tendeth. Every
> cause is in the effect which groweth from it. Our souls
> and bodies quickened to eternal life are effects the cause
> whereof is the Person of Christ, his body and his blood
> are the true well-spring out of which this life floweth.
> (Book 5. LXVII. 5)

For Hooker, the ultimate location of the presence of Christ's
body and blood is not to be sought in the sacrament, but
rather 'in the worthy receiver ... only in the very heart and
soul of him which receiveth him.' This might appear to be
rather bland at first sight, but it is far from that. The key to
Hooker's sacramental theology lies not in the minutiae of
the Reformation debates about the real presence, but rather
in the essence of 'participation', which he calls 'the fruit of
the Eucharist'. This participation flows from his dynamic
and organic ecclesiology. For Hooker, participation is not
over-prescribed or narrow, but is rather public and corpo-
rate, and is the key to individual and social life intricately
wrapped within the life of God.

Correspondingly, he is wonderfully diplomatic in his treatment of competing doctrines of the Eucharist that dominated
the debates of his day. In chapter 67 (LXVII) of Book 5, he
gives space to air the three main theories on Christ's presence
in the bread and wine. But Hooker has the last word, using a
phrase that resonates with his warning in the Preface that 'our
safest eloquence concerning him is our silence':

He which hath said of the one sacrament [i.e., baptism], 'wash and clean', hath said concerning the other likewise [i.e., the Eucharist], 'eat and live'. If therefore without any such particular and solemn warrant as this is that poor distressed woman coming unto Christ for health could so constantly resolve herself, 'may I but touch the skirt of his garment I shall be made whole,' what moveth us to argue the manner of how life should by bread, our duty being here to take what is offered, and most surely to rest persuaded of this? . . . Let it therefore be sufficient for me presenting myself at the Lord's table to know that what there I receive from him, without searching or inquiring of the manner how Christ performeth his promise; let disputes and questions, enemies to piety . . . let them take their rest . . .. (Book 5. LXVII.12)

Here, Hooker reveals himself as an explicit conciliator, only demolishing arguments in order to make peace and bring about a wider form of ecclesial participation. As a form of apologetics, it is a model for all those who seek to hold together competing convictions, and seek to promote unity in the face of polarisation.

Power, Ministry and Politics
Mutuality and consent characterise Hooker's theorising on legitimate ministries and the rightful use of political power.

I could easily declare how all things which are of God he hath by wonderful art and wisdom so ordered as it were with the glue of mutual assistance, appointing the lowest to receive from the nearest to themselves what the influence of the highest yieldeth. And therefore the Church being the most absolute of all his works was in reason to be also ordered with like harmony, that what he worketh might no less in grace then in nature be effected by hands and instruments duly subordinated unto the power of his own spirit. (Book 5. LXXVI. 9)

Book 5 is mainly concerned with ministry, and although issues of power often crop up (in questions of liturgy, order and the like), they are usually implicit and incidental. However, Books 6-8 of *The Laws* are explicitly concerned with authority and power. At the outset of this brief section, it should be noted that these three books were published posthumously, and there is some debate as to how much they have been corrupted. What can be safely said is that very substantial drafts were written by Hooker, and an outline written in 1593 by the author suggests that the three volumes were near completion. It is not clear what delayed their posthumous publication, although Puritan suppression during the English Civil War seems likely.

The burden of these three remaining books is: (1) a rejection of lay elders; (2) a defence of episcopacy; and (3) a defence of the monarch as the head of the Church. In the matter of lay elders, Hooker adopts a classic Anglican line, namely noting and describing how 'ministers' are those set aside by Christ for the Church, and in turn, these same ministers have particular tasks – especially in the field of confession and absolution – that set them apart from the laity, but not above them.

On the episcopacy, Hooker is more circumspect. He adopts a traditionalist view of bishops, declaring them to be appointed by the apostles. Correspondingly, bishops may hold power over their ministers by virtue of their duties and callings. However, that said, Hooker also recognises that the power of a bishop is held consensually within the Church (it 'hath the power by universal consent ... to take it away'), and that the upholding of the tradition of translation of apostolic power to episcopal power rests upon a law of reason. Here, Hooker is a moderate: he readily recognises that legitimate polity may exist without bishops or kings, since, in his view, it is the individual who is crowned or consecrated, not the office. In other words, bishops are beneficial, but they are not indispensable (Book 7. III).

Finally, Book 8 deals with the question of monarchy. Here the discussion of power, religion and civic life reaches its climax in Hooker's participative ideology, that identifies the Church as the body within society that holds 'true religion' for the State. For Hooker, there can be no separation of the two: they are inexorably entwined. According to Hooker, to belong to the Church of England is to belong to the Commonwealth, and to belong to that society is to be part of the Church. Put simply, saints and citizens, though they are different, none the less work under the same laws which govern all politic societies, who in turn derive their being from God (1.6: McGrade, pp. 137ff.).

This is an important observation, for just as Hooker's participative sacramental theology permits a plural Church, so does his participative view of Church and society permit 'Church and commonwealth' a certain amount of say in one another's affairs. It is in this context that a monarch may exercise power in the Church. But as with bishops, Hooker is quick to remind his readers that they do not make the laws, but rather impart them:

> Happier the people whose law is their king in the greatest things, than those whose King is himself their law. Where the King doth guide the state and the law the King, that commonwealth is like an harp or melodious instrument, the strings whereof are tuned and handled all by one hand, following as laws the rules and canons or musical science. (3.3: McGrade, pp. 146-7).

Once again, we are back to 'rules for goodness', harmony, melody and unity of purpose. *The Laws of Ecclesiastical Polity* end as they begin, seeking to knit religion and the world, Church and society, into one body that is governed graciously by the laws of God for the common good.

Why Read Richard Hooker?
(With Canon Trevor Page)

It has already been noted that reading Richard Hooker is far from easy. The density of language, archaic rhetorical structures and devices, coupled with improbably long sentences, require the full attention of the reader. And yet that is precisely the place to begin to appreciate Hooker. Hooker is a demanding but rewarding read, not least because his apologetic and rhetorical style manage to convey the beauty and truth of Anglicanism. His pleas for tolerance are matched by a patience in language. His appeals to the breadth of God's laws are complemented by an instructive depth and colour in his argument.

The modern study of rhetoric has done much to draw our attention to the power of words in the art of persuasion. From Northrop Frye to Richard Rorty, and from Brian Vickers to Kenneth Burke, literary critics and philosophers have discovered afresh how arguments are won and lost by the careful selection and modelling of words. Hooker is one of the best exponents of the art, and provides a pattern of speech that can inform an ordinary sermon as much as a weighty debate. Whilst the style is now dated, the actual form behind it is timeless: there is a rhythmic, almost musical resonance to his words, making passages more than memorable, and actually imprinting them on the soul. He preaches wisdom.

So, at the outset, Hooker can inform students and scholars on how to structure an argument, and how to grace apologetics with artful rhetoric that can persuade and influence. In this sense, one can learn as much from Hooker as one can from reading the sermons of Andrewes or Laud.

Hooker also matters because he mattered to John Keble and the other nineteenth-century revivalists. If Anglicanism has any contribution to make to national revival and self-renewal, it must be in the demonstration of what it is to worship the Lord in the beauty of holiness. Hooker had a profound grasp of this (Book 5), and any student of Hooker lives perpetually with a heightened awareness of the possibilities of worship.

> Between the throne of God in heaven and his church upon earth here militant if it be so that Angels have their continual intercourse, where should we find the same more verified than in these two ghostly exercises, the one Doctrine and the other Prayer? For what is the assembling of the church to learn, but the receiving of Angels descended from above? What to pray but the sending of Angels upwards? His heavenly aspirations and our holy desires as so many Angels of intercourse and commerce between God and us. (Book 5.XXIII.1)

Keble saw that from Hooker's vital sense of holiness in worship, there sprang a strong renewing sense of the sacramental, in which outward formal rituals can be freshly appreciated as sources of blessing from God and response from humanity.

Hooker also matters because a Church with a weakened sense of tradition, or one with which it is ill at ease, has much to learn from one who saw Christian living as a constant interplay between the four elements of Scripture, tradition, sensation and reason. We retain a high regard for Scripture and a high regard for present experience, though not always in necessarily reasonable forms. All too often contemporary Anglicanism tends to bring scriptural texts directly to bear on questions, as if two thousand years of scriptural living had produced no visible benefit, guidelines or wisdom at all. Scriptural literalism and suspicion of tradition today create precisely the same conditions that Hooker sought to correct. If tradition is neither known nor valued, then the Scriptures themselves can neither be read nor applied with any safety.

For Hooker, Scripture was primary: all his writings are suffused with scriptural quotation. But Scripture, he argues, lives in us through the application of reason upon it. Reason here was not seen as mere intellectual ability. By reason, Hooker implied the sum of the Christian's experience, not in its own right, but as a setting for the gift of grace. Reason is the God-given ability to focus this experience of grace upon the Scripture and tradition presented to us.

Correspondingly, worship is the centre of experience; grace is at the centre of worship. By reason, the experience of grace in the Church is brought to bear upon Scripture and tradition. And that application implies no common democracy in which one person's views are equal to another. It belongs to those who have authority for judgement on behalf of others. Scripture, then, is primary; but it can only be properly understood through the application of reason, and then illuminated by grace within the life of the Church. And the tradition in which Scripture was formed, and which has then been formed by Scripture, is a fundamental element binding together the life of the Church.

Hooker's writings are steeped in quotation from the early fathers. He certainly knew his own age, but he entered into his age breathing the air of those centuries when the canon of Scripture was formed, and the great creeds agreed. It is that sense of living out of tradition which is so powerful. Too often today, 'tradition' is merely acknowledged; it is regarded as a rather detached body of case law that might be consulted in times of need or crisis. Yet Hooker's fundamental appeal to law reminds the contemporary Church that the 'principles of God' are dispersed, not concentrated. The task of the

Church is to gather and articulate these principles, and then offer them to society, mindful that they neither belong to the Church nor to society, but to the author and peacemaker of our common good.

It is sometimes said that the Anglican Church venerates Hooker through its very divisions, in that Evangelicals stress Scripture, Anglo-Catholics tradition, and Liberals reason, and others still experience. For Hooker, what is essential in the holding together of all four elements in working harmony is their lawful integrity, derived from their source, namely God. It is the sense of all four integrated – in worship, doctrine and Christian and civic life – that is close to the heart of Anglicanism. It is a living working unity. Reason is applied to Scripture in the humility that sees Scripture as primary. At the same time, reason is freshly formed out of our gracious life within a Church which, again in humility, looks to its tradition as authoritative. It is all rather mysterious, very much about harmony, very Trinitarian. This music is the true tenor of Anglicanism.

Hooker is worthy of attention today, not least because a principal concern of his was how a civil religion could best enhance a civic society. Hooker saw that to live under law was to live within the divine economy. Furthermore, that human flourishing was a fundamental task of the Church, as laws in all their forms were there for the whole of public life, in order that society could live peaceably together in its plurality. But Hooker's laws are never to be imposed on society; they are offered to the world in much the same way that Christ is given. As Hooker says:

> Behold therefore we offer the laws whereby we live unto the general trial and judgement of the whole world; heartily beseeching almighty God, whom we desire to serve according to his own will, that both we and others (all kinds of partial affection being laid clean aside) may

have eyes to see and hearts to embrace the things that in his sight are most acceptable. (Book 1.I.3)

Conclusion:
Anglicanism after Hooker
An Essay on Future Possibilities

The state of the monarchy is the supremest thing upon earth; for kings are not only God's lieutenants upon earth, and sit upon God's throne, but even by himself they are called gods. In the scriptures, kings are called gods, and so their power after certain relation compared to the divine power. Kings are also compared to fathers of families: for a king is truly *parens patriae*, the politic father of his people. And lastly kings are compared to the head of this microcosm of the body of man ...

> James I of England, Speech in Whitehall Palace,
> 21 March 1609.

As for judicial authority to punish malefactors, if the King be as the kings of Israel were, and as every of ours is a supreme Lord than whom none under God is by way of ruling authority and higher power where he reigneth, how should any there have the high place of a judge over him?

> Hooker, *The Laws*, Book 8, Chapter 9: 6.

The Church of England that Hooker knew and contended for is a very different body some four hundred years later. Hooker wrote before a worldwide Anglican Communion ever existed. Furthermore, his vision of law and Church is distinctively English, even though it has classical roots. Hooker knew little of Europe, at least insofar as its existence as a union of united states might come to question the whole nature of Establishment, power and politics in relation to religion in England.

One apparent major problem with reading Hooker at the turn of the Millennium is that the 'polity' he strove for feels backward looking and outdated. Few theologians would defend the role of the monarch as 'head of the Church', save only in a symbolic sense. Equally, it is hard to see how such an English socio-political and ecclesial programme of the kind that Hooker knew could flourish in the face of progressive European union. The emergence of Europe, and the re-placement of Britain (or more specifically, England), has yet to find its way to the top of the theological agenda. Yet the combination of subsidiarity (decisions taken at the most local level), regionalisation (normally for the purposes of regeneration) and federalism, removes both power and influence from their traditional locations. Rights, laws and development grants can flow just as easily from Brussels and The Hague as they might from Westminster. One 'centre' of government, symbolised (or even actualised) by a monarch, has given way to a plurality of centres that carry different weights and authority.

The mere fact of this poses a threat to English 'theological autonomy'. The Church of England can no longer simply secure its business and will through 'the Establishment' (the House of Lords, the monarchy and the House of Commons). Instead, it must attend to a wider set of principles that will almost inevitably come to bear on the English society that the Church of England serves and shapes. As I write, some bishops in the House of Lords have recently lost an amendment that would have excluded churches from the Bill of Human Rights. On the other hand, only a month later, the same group managed to win out against equalising the age of consent for homosexuals, maintaining consensual gay sex at sixteen and seventeen (between men) as a criminal offence (the law does not prescribe for lesbians here). Both votes caused something of a stir in the media and in the churches, between May to July 1998.

What is interesting about these two events is that clearly it exposes how different the 'Establishment' that Hooker envisaged – complete with binding socio-ecclesial laws that had divine roots – is from that we know today. The voting in the House of Lords can have no enduring impact, since Britain would be breaking European law if it did not adopt the rights and equalisation legislation by 1999. Britain is a voluntary signatory to European conventions, that binds its laws (and eventually its conventions, currency and the like) to its European neighbours. Add to this the increasing regionalisation of Britain (Assemblies for Wales and Northern Ireland, and a Parliament for Scotland), and we can speak meaningfully of a new cultural political situation: aristocracy making way for meritocracy, autocracy for democracy.

In such a situation, Hooker's defence of a monarch closely related to the Church and to politics looks quaint but irrelevant. Furthermore, that one Church (of England) now finds itself in a decidedly odd position, since representing the nation (only England?) is a different matter to that which Hooker understood. Closer European ecclesial ties also question Anglican polity. In one sense, the Porvoo Agreement is a kind of theological Maastricht, subtly alerting the historic and apostolic understandings of episcopal power through a new covenant. Beyond this, Anglicanism has steadily evolved into a global communion (since the American Revolution of 1776), in which the Church of England is now but one part: it has no monopoly on the meanings of polity.

All these comments appear to make Hooker virtually redundant. Yet on the contrary, I wish to suggest that his work is now ripe for rehabilitation. There are three reasons for this. First, Hooker's concept of 'law' is surprisingly reflexive and postmodern. Hooker appears to offer a meta-narrative (law) that dominates his discourse and its subjects. In actual fact, his proposition is that laws are, at least in part, *with* and *for* the people rather than just over them. His stress on consensual power and goodness as a benchmark for weighing law is practical. He also has a doctrine of development that allows laws to be changed and constructed from a plurality of sources.

Second, Hooker believed in laws affecting 'the common-weal': as we noted earlier, his term for the totality of an organic society. Hooker was in no rush to divorce the sacred from the secular, and he resisted Congregationalist theologies that sought to separate Church from society and the State. Hooker counted all in society as members of the Church, for the Church was only a part of God's world.

Third, Hooker saw that power in leadership, politics and in the episcopacy depended on a degree of consensual participation. Although Hooker defends hegemony, he also constantly checks this by appealing to higher laws that require power to be rightful and shared. In this sense, Hooker was a subtle reformer of the Establishment. He believed both in the centralisation of power and in its dispersal. Absolute power belonged only to God; and even God, in his wisdom, chose many ways of offering it to the world. Hooker was nervous of power being narrowed, concentrated and directed: the apologia against the Puritans is an appeal to the breadth of God's self-disclosure.

From the Church of England to the Anglican Family

J. Gordon Melton, in his *Encyclopaedia of Religion in the USA* (First Edition, 1978), categorises expressions of American religious life according to 'families'. He identifies at least seventeen different families, of which Anglicanism features as just one branch within the 'Liturgical Family (Western)'. In choosing to adopt the word 'family' to describe expressions of religion, Melton is arguing for a structural understanding of religion that achieves two goals. First, it permits him to reject the simplistic European-centred distinctions of Troeltsch between 'church', 'sect' and 'cult', which are potentially pejorative, besides being artificial and sometimes clumsy. Second, it therefore allows religious expressions to be grouped together according to their ecclesial, social and doctrinal similarity, not according to size or social impact. Undoubtedly, there are some benefits in this approach, but it is not without its weaknesses.

As fundamentalists have known for nearly a century, and are now joined by one or two Anglican groups, many of their 'family members' (or kin) often do not recognise each another, let alone talk to one another. The reason for the proliferation of 'family members' in ecclesiastical history is not usually expansion, nor the indigenous enculturation of imported or exported religious tradition. It is much more likely to occur because of a breakdown in relationships, perhaps caused by disagreements over authority, interpretation or personality-clashes, simple rebellion, or even open hostility.

Melton's 'family' analogy is appealing for a number of reasons. First, it is close to Hooker's idea of the Church as 'kinship'. It is also a better way of describing the complexity of Anglicanism at all levels in late modernity. The problem with a metaphor such as 'body of Christ' is that its oneness is assumed too easily, and discussion gets too quickly to rhetoric such as 'head', 'parts' and other ciphers for structural re-ordering. Whilst Hooker believed in rightful hegemony, it is important to remember that he also affirms the right and power of subjects to question and reject a 'head', which is why he sometimes prefers familial language for his ecclesiology.

The family analogy still allows us to keep a 'head' (the

bishop as father in God, or perhaps a monarch as another kind of 'head' of the Church, symbolising political and ecclesial partnership for social wellbeing and flourishing), but taps into the richer but more implicit New Testament concept of *oikos* – the household of faith. In a family, there are resemblances and differences. Families mature and age, but there is also new life. And practically speaking families are very difficult to manage. Some members will specialise in finance: others will be lousy at it. Some will be outstanding in their sociability; others almost reclusive. Yet in spite of differentiation, there is a sense of belonging.

The advantage of beginning an ecclesiology for the Church with the concept of family is that it permits pluralism and particularity, yet also respects unity of purpose, function and order. In a family, management is never for its own sake, but is for the other members. Also, the model of family does offer some potential for clarity of structure. For example, whilst a family would normally attend to the views and needs of all its members, it does not follow that all the members run the family, or that the family is run for any particular one of them. This is not the thin end of the wedge in reinventing hegemony. Rather, it is simply to say that the task of leadership resides with those who are charged with fulfilling that vocation.

According to one theologian, if you give any group of Anglicans a couple of topics to discuss, they will inevitably spend the greater time and energy on the more trivial of the two. Given a choice between mission to the parish and the new colour stain for the pews, seating will win every time. Or given a choice between matters of pastoral or theological gravity versus rotas and rosters, it is not difficult to see where most of the effort will be directed. I conclude with three common concerns for Anglicans, which Hooker would doubtless still affirm as vital issues, and to some extent, is still capable of answering.

The first of these concerns the true nature of communion. Anglicanism is the second largest global communion in the world. As such, it is a genuine commonwealth of belief and practice. Bringing order to this diversity is difficult, and probably not desirable. American bishops don't always see eye to eye with their African counterparts on a whole range of gender and sexuality issues. But then the communion is a commonwealth, so agreement in all things might feel a bit repressive. Diversity, far from being a recipe for disunity, may in fact be a reflection of divinity.

Participation is the key. The concept of communion should be a celebration of pluralism and diversity, not an apology for divergence. It really doesn't matter that the bishops don't always agree: it would be rather odd if they did. Much of the doctrine of the Church comes from hard-fought struggle, which is, of course, ongoing. But there is usually an eventual convergence, a common and directional plurality in which people of differing views and integrities move together towards God's future.

The second of these concerns relates to the collegiality of the Church. A 'college' is a place where difference is attractive and constructive, provided it serves a common purpose. At present, the Church of England seems to be torn between two polarised models of collegiality. One of these versions seeks to run the Church like a PLC, run by a board and a chief executive. The other is the more familiar 'medieval court' model, in which prelates preside as feudal lords over priests and laity. Hooker would not have inclined to either. Moreover, it is generally accepted that the culture of monarchy has moved from one of 'divine right' to one where 'it exists only by the will and consent of the people' (Elizabeth II, 7 September 1997).

The Church of England has as much to learn from the changing face of monarchical government as it does from its Anglican brothers and sisters in other parts of the world.

In some countries, collegiality has been made to work by dispersing power, not concentrating it. Bishops share in the task of leadership. More democratic and accountable systems of governance have meant a common ownership of the Church, in which, again, difference and diversity are valued assets, not signs of weakness or division.

Third, a celebration of the comprehensiveness of Anglicanism is long overdue. The Anglican Communion is a broad Church, and is intended to be a genuinely inclusive body. The wideness of God's mercy should be reflected in the Church; narrowing the love of God should be avoided. When the Anglican Church lives like this, it can afford to celebrate its breadth which is its life, and move forward with confidence in a new Millennium. However, that move can only come if it continues to attend to its true vocation, namely to be the Church for the unchurched, the Church for all people. The body that is everywhere for those who feel they are nowhere. To be a place of belief for the many who do so, yet may choose not to belong.

The foundations of a true communion – a form of family – lie in recognising that power should ideally be dispersed, and works best when it is shared. In any case, power in a family is subject to flux and flow. Such a vision sees interdependency as a necessary condition for Church life that should be cherished. Furthermore, it encourages rightful hegemony, with the express will and consent of the participants in a given community. Rather than permanently concentrating power in one office or body, we need to create systems of exchange and empowerment that foster the federation (family), enable subsidiarity to flourish, yet are ultimately focused and directed for the common good which seeks to support the whole of society.

Hooker's vision for the Church and for society, although a child of its time and context, still speaks with power today. Furthermore, it does so not just to England, but to the

Anglican Communion and the societies they serve as a whole. Although Hooker writes in a partisan manner against Puritans and other separatists, his purpose is always deeper. He seeks coherence in society, and to foster a situation in which people of differing views – ecclesiastical, social and political – can co-exist peacefully and harmoniously. Although a doughty defender of the monarchy and the established Church, his own appeal to his audience lies beyond this. There may be 'great reason' to observe and obey laws; there may well be 'no necessity' to criticise them (Pref. 7.1). Yet Hooker also knows that the acceptance of law is a matter of willing participation in a given communal order.

Ultimately, this sets a new tone for Anglicanism. One in which the *modus operandi* and *modus vivendi* assume as much importance as the laws and articles of faith that bind a Church together. *How* you believe your faith is as important as *what* you believe: how you *disagree* in faith is as important as the matter in dispute. Hooker understood this, and he stands in a long line of gentle Anglican theologians who sought not revolution, but reformation; and to argue by persuasion, not force. This suggests that 'tradition' is no longer to be regarded as concrete and static, but more of a gel. It still holds things together, but is flexible and responsive to the contours it seeks to support and enhance, for the sake of the world and the Church. And in the name of the living God.

Why Be an Anglican?
A Sermon for Students on
Richard Hooker Day,
3 November 1996

The Church of England is an object of ridicule. Badly organised, out of date, it is often said that it could not organise its way out of a paper bag without a committee to deliberate and defer. It is too beholden to its past. Moreover, its congregations are generally unfriendly, elitist and out of touch – not God's chosen people so much as frozen people – stuck in a time warp. Jokes about Anglicans are a dime a dozen.

So, why be an Anglican at all? Some of you will know my predilection for following lost causes, like supporting Everton football club. Isn't the Church of England just another one of those mistakes? Surely putting money on a sober dinner with the choir would be a safer bet?

For some time now, many people have been claiming that the Church of England is dying. Some recent statistics appear to confirm their suspicions. They show a drop in the number of Anglican worshippers, the total falling perilously close to that million mark. The blame is laid at the door of boring services, out-of-touch clergy, and 'traditionalists' who pride themselves too much on aesthetics. So much so, in fact, that it is culturally elite – far removed from ordinary life.

Then again, others claim that the Church of England is dying of the very opposite. Happy-clappy songs and trite forms of worship turn people off. In ignoring beauty, art and a theology of any substance, 'trendies' offer a culturally-relevant version of the gospel that can self-destruct. It is always in vogue, but ultimately disposable; religion comes as a fashion accessory, not a necessity So, what we have here is a record – turning about 1 rpm (one revolution per millennium) – with two sides to it.

Side A – '*traditionalists*' – prefer a church with neatly turned out priests in ornate seasonal sacramental robes (purple is in at the moment). Congregations sit in heavy oak pews, and glory in feeling subdued and sublime. There is good music, and scholarly sermons.

Side B – '*trendies*' – prefer pastors who look like game show hosts, and wander round the congregation with a roving microphone, asking believers about their religious experience of the week. A sort of Christian televisual magazine; the congregation relaxes in comfy chairs, applauding God now and then.

Behind the argument over taste, there are more serious concerns. Anglicanism is not an argument for the superiority of Schubert over The Spice Girls. The issue is one of substance. Modes of worship provide a barometer for analysis: there may be a link between theological and aesthetic vacuity, or elitism and 'high' Anglican culture, and the declining number of communicants. In preferring hymns like 'Thine be the Glory' to choruses that offer sentiments such as 'Lord, I Just Want to Cuddle You', the issue is as much about theology as it is about taste. The latter type of song 'domesticates' God, turning 'Praise the Lord in the Beauty of Holiness' into 'I Acknowledge You in a Fashion-conscious Medium'.

Are either of the parties right? Have church numbers declined due to good taste or bad religion? Or is it just public indifference? At first sight, the squabble over taste in worship seems about as useful as third class passengers arguing with first class passengers over the colour scheme for the *Titanic*. Religion has good and bad bits in it – always has – but the ship still seems to be going down. Is anyone or anything to blame?

Churches that appear to be successful, packing the pews with a slick message, smoochy choruses and with upbeat hymns, might actually be *eroding* people's faith. This is so because the churches don't offer any real theological breadth or depth. The worship is anodyne and escapist, an opiate for the urban Christian. The services are cheap and cheerful, albeit for the sake of conversion. But once people have become bored with this bargain basement religion, they chuck the product away. Some Anglicans fear they have been cheated – they've never actually tried the real thing. Hence this assault on this brand of pirate religion. The warning is this: don't buy cheap imitations.

None the less, all have to work together, so what is to be done? For a start, both sides could address themselves to the problem that is in hand – an alleged fall in church attendance. The statisticians should be their target, for the gloss placed on the decline in numbers clearly suffers from what some have dubbed (in a somewhat sexist manner) 'the Dolly Parton Syndrome': a large figure, blown up out of all proportion, with no visible means of support. Alarmist statistics are very misleading. Church attendance in Britain has always been in a state of flux. But the power of religion lies in its capacity to influence society, not just in the number of punters turning out on Sunday. Only *some* figures tell a story of decline, but millions still believe in God, and opt for a Christian burial. The impact of Christian belief in Britain remains highly pervasive and persuasive.

But there are deeper issues beyond this for Anglican faith. For to make a claim over the 'essence' of Anglicanism is to miss its point. Anglicans are a funny bunch of folk:

high, low, medium; charismatic, liberal – even one or two 'don't knows'. Anglicanism is a plural faith, encompassing many different expressions of Christian faith. Initially, that is what appeals to me about Anglicanism. You can't easily pin it down, define it, articulate it – it is too big, broad, mysterious. Like God. From this vision, Anglicans try and hold their churches together in at least three ways:

1. An understanding that the Bible, tradition, culture and reason all have a part to play in governing the Church and deciding doctrine. We all make decisions differently, weighing each side of the equation.

2. A belief in sociality – a Church for people, not just members. It is no accident that the C of E offers a type of 'comprehensive National Church Service' – you're in, unless you opt out. This is, in my view, a sign of God's graciousness and comprehensive love, rather than a 'catch-all' weak-liberal policy. The Church offers its services to all because it believes God loves all – not just believers.

3. A commitment to coolness. Alan Bennett says, in *Writing Home*, that 'an enthusiastic Anglican is a contradiction in terms'. He is sort of right. Anglicanism prides itself on its coolness and its rationality. It tries to think before it speaks. But, it is an engaged kind of coolness that is held with passion, which is why bishops do get involved in politics, challenge the Establishment, and argue. It is why theologians push for changes in society. . .and the Church.

In short, the kind of God I believe in is a reflection of a broad and catholic Anglican faith. A God who is big enough to let us choose, travel and journey in belief, using our minds and hearts, as well as faith and feeling. A God who does not coerce or compel faith, but rather offers it. A God who loves and cares for all, not just the faithful. A God who is committed to society, and is decidedly passionate, but also cool. A God who does not overwhelm us. He wants us to mature in life and faith. So, I'm not an Anglican for the

Prayer Book, although I love this type of worship for its capacity to enable sublime participation in God. I'm not an Anglican because I am especially pro-Establishment, although I think the Church should participate fully in society, and society fully in the Church. I'm an Anglican by sheer conviction, believing it to offer a profound and liberating model of God and the Church for the world in which we live.

I know it has it faults: all bodies do. But Anglicanism above all aspires to be an incarnational body. That is to say, a body of Christ that is deliberately open and ambiguous, and yet strangely defined and delimited. It offers power, yet can be powerless; it offers hope, yet can be, at times, hopeless. I think God gave of himself in Jesus Christ in exactly this way, which is why, for me, to be an Anglican is a deep and valid form of Christianity: it is tragic, comic, ironic and romantic – but above all, it tries to be true to a real God, and true to real life.

Questions

A. *Hooker's Life and Context*
1. How does 'Puritan' thought continue to threaten the Church of England?
2. Why is the combination of patience and passion in apologetics so appealing?
3. To what extent is Hooker constructing a *via media*?

B. *The Laws: A Brief Outline*
1. Why does Hooker think that reform is 'neither possible, nor certain, nor absolutely convenient', and then advocate a doctrine of development?
2. Hooker aims at wooing separatists: to what extent can apologetics achieve unity and harmony?
3. What is the attraction of literalism?

C. *Reading Hooker*
1. How useful are Hooker's distinctions of laws for today's Church?
2. Does the quadrilateral model succeed in maintaining unity and difference or is it just 'the Dodo's incorporative principle' (Robert Carroll)?
3. How sustainable is an organic ecclesiology in an atomised society?

D. *Why Read Hooker Today?*
1. How would attention to rhetoric be beneficial in ministerial formation?
2. In what ways can a civil religion help form a civic society?

3. Can 'tradition' be taught, or only caught?

E. *Anglicanism after Hooker*
1. How might the Church of England be affected by the transformation of 'Establishment'?
2. What does closer European union mean for those Churches that are established in member states?
3. Will perceptions of episcopacy be changed as traditional forms of government (e.g., the House of Lords) are altered?

References

PRIMARY SOURCES:

The Laws of Ecclesiastical Polity, edited by Christopher Morris (London: J. M. Dent, 1907, Everyman edition – Books 1–5 only, plus sermons).

The Works of that Learned and Judicious Divine Mr Richard Hooker: With an Account of his Life and Death by Izaak Walton, edited by John Keble (Oxford: Clarendon, 1888).

The Laws of Ecclesiastical Polity: An Abridged Edition, edited by A. S. McGrade and B. Vickers (New York: St Martin's Press, 1975).

The Laws of Ecclesiastical Polity, edited by A. McGrade (Cambridge, CUP, 1989, Cambridge series, contains Preface, Books 1 & 8).

The Folger Library Edition of the Works of Richard Hooker, edited by W. Speed Hill (Cambridge: Harvard University Press, 1977-82) 6 volumes.

SECONDARY SOURCES:

Archer, S., *Richard Hooker* (Boston: Twayne Press, 1983).

Atkinson, N., *Richard Hooker and the Authority of Scripture, Tradition and Reason* (Carlisle: Paternoster, 1998).

Davies, E., *The Political Ideas of Richard Hooker* (London: SPCK, 1948).

Marshall, S., *Hooker and the Anglican Tradition* (Sewanee, Tenn.: University of the South Press, 1963).

Pollard, A., *Richard Hooker* (London: Longman, Green & Co., 1966).

Thornton, L., *Richard Hooker: A Study of his Theology* (London: SPCK, 1924).